I0134973

Make a Spectacular Seashell Lamp

Everything you Need to Know

by

J.D. Monk

Monk Publications

Copyright ©2022 Judy Bidgood All rights reserved

No part of this book may be reproduced, stored in a retrieval system, or transmitted in any form or by any means electronic or mechanical, or by photocopying, recording, or otherwise, without express written permission of the author.

TABLE OF CONTENTS

ACKNOWLEDGEMENTS

I'd like to thank my husband John, who helped plan and arrange our unforgettable trips to Turks and Caicos, and Greater Exuma, Bahamas, where I gleaned most of my shell collections. Each lamp is a testament not only to nature's beauty, but to the lifelong memories we collected along the way.

Thanks to my daughter Marlee, who provided her valuable time and expertise in helping to format this e-book and lessen the frustration of a not-so-techno-savvy mom. My daughters Carolyn and Jayne provided encouragement throughout the process.

INTRODUCTION

A beautiful seashell lamp is not only an expression of creativity but a testament to your passion for shelling and your love of nature. Your creation may even become a family heirloom, cherished by loved ones for years to come.

If you are like me, you are an avid collector of beach treasure: seashells, sea glass, stones, maybe some driftwood. Bringing some of that treasure home can remind us again and again of those carefree, pleasant times on the beach.

Tar Bay viewed through a Casuarina Tree in Exuma

My best seashell collecting has been in Greater Exuma, a district in The Bahamas, where my husband and I spent weeks walking the glorious beaches. Often, ours were the only footprints in the sand. The turquoise water where you could walk out long distances and still be only shin deep, and that pristine white sand, made me feel as though I was in paradise.

Some years were better than others for shelling. This past January, following Hurricane Dorian, I noticed a big difference in the sea's offerings. There were many tiny shells this year, and far fewer of the medium or larger shells. We found lots of sea

3

fans strewn about the inner shores, more than other years. Further on in the book, I offer tips on how to more easily find shells when it seems that there are 'none'.

Crashing Surf at Tar Bay

The first year we visited Exuma, we stayed in a charming, brightly-painted cottage on the ocean. On a living room table stood a beautiful seashell lamp, not something I had ever before seen. It was the focal point of the room and I knew I had to make one for our own home. As you might imagine, this gave me a whole new purpose for my daily shelling adventures.

That first year, we found a large variety of shells on Tar Bay, especially sunrise tellin clam shells. At Cocoplum Beach, you can walk far out onto the sandbars at low tide. This beach is also known as Sand Dollar Beach, for good reason. Here we delighted in reaching into the shallow water to gently extract gleaming white sand dollars. See my tips below for gentle extraction and packing of sand dollars, including how to spot sand dollars that are still alive (because we must leave those where they lie).

We also found starfish, bubble shells, flamingo tongue, Scotch bonnet, lettered olive, Atlantic sundial, cowrie helmet, shark's eye, scallop, cockle, buttercup lucine, and many others featured in my shell lamp. The finely branched white corals that are so useful as finishing touches were found in a bay near Jolly Hall Beach, called Palm Bay. It's interesting how seashells gather in certain areas over others. One thing that doesn't change, though, is that each time I go shelling is just as exciting as the first.

View from the Verandah at Casuarina House

This section looks Full and Rich, with lots of 'Movement'.

1. A FEW TIPS ON FINDING, COLLECTING, AND PROTECTING

Check the Tide Tables

Find out when the tide is low; it may be well worth the wait. Obviously, shells are easier to find at low tide, and they may be easier to pick up if the ocean is rough. All the better if you can be the first person on the beach.

When the tide is high, shells can be found in less obvious places. For example, on my last trip I discovered many beauties, including starfish, secured in a tangle of sea grass swept to shore. A vigorous high tide can reap rewards for those who are willing to venture forth when the opportunity arises, taking a quick look, perhaps a quick pick-up before the next wave threatens to knock you off your feet.

Protect your Shells

Put some thought into what you will bring to the beach to collect your finds and protect them from breakage. This is particularly important regarding sand dollars, sea urchins, starfish, doubles (both top and bottom of a clam shell, for example), and other delicate finds.

I have found sand dollars to be the most difficult shells to bring home safely. I'll never forget the delight of finding a gleaming white sand dollar in calm, shallow water on a sunny and clear-blue-sky day. As I reached for it with great anticipation, it completely crumbled in my hand. Yes, they are much more delicate and fragile than they look. Now, I approach my pickup differently. What works for me is this: I dig under the sand dollar a bit and keep my hand flat as I emerge from the water with my prize intact. Then I place it carefully in whatever I have brought that day to help protect my most delicate pieces. Bubble wrap seems to work well most of the time. Occasionally, however, I have placed several sand dollars, one on top of the other, in just a zip-lock bag, and they have survived the journey somewhat. I may have tissue inside a tin can or plastic container, or just whatever I have been able to find in our cottage rental. From home, I bring bubble wrap, plastic bags and containers, sometimes small but sturdy carboard boxes. In my early days of collecting, I simply wrapped my finds in tissue and newspaper, resulting in broken pieces. You need containers that can withstand heavy blows through airline baggage handling. I bring onboard my most special finds, but there is only so much room allowed.

I learned something new on my last trip to the Caribbean. I gathered some seagrass found on the shore and wrapped it around shells, then I inserted the lot into my containers. That worked out very well, and I was able to transport my finds safely to the car.

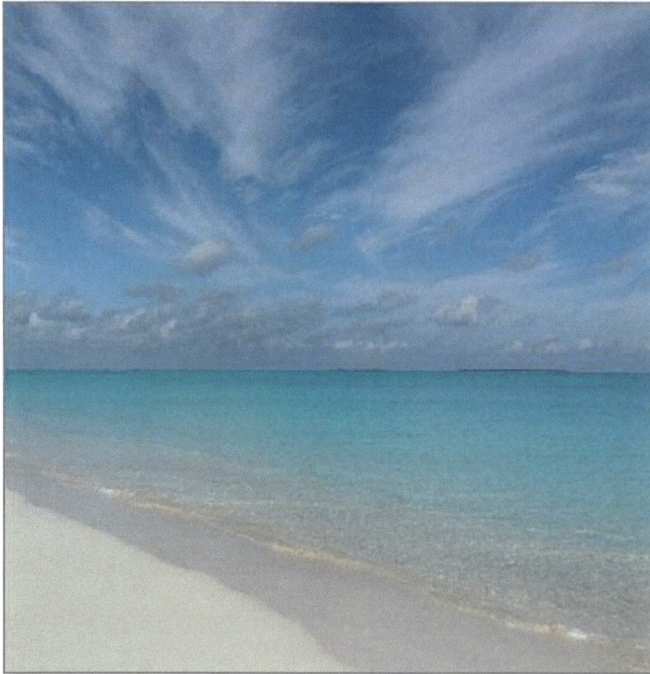

Packing for Travel

Fragile shells travel best with cushioning inside sturdy containers. I find that the best cushioning is provided by bubble wrap, although less fragile shells can travel well wrapped in just tissue and/or newspaper. I have transported lots of small shells in empty spice bottles without any cushioning at all. These small plastic or glass bottles can fit inside shoes, etc., for extra protection. The trick is to pack your containers full to minimize movement. I find empty vegetable or fruit cans to be fairly damage resistant, although their size can be quite restrictive.

Ethical Collecting

It's good to know how to tell if your sea creature is alive or dead so you don't accidentally kill any living animal. Sand dollars should be bleached white and without any tiny, bristly 'hairs' or spines. If it is brown and velvety looking, then it's probably alive, especially if the tiny hairs are moving, so return it to the ocean.

On the underside of each arm of a starfish, check for moving tentacles. As an extra precaution, gently touch the tentacles or place the starfish in the water to see if there is any movement.

If you find a sea urchin with spines attached, it may be alive. Check inside; if the shell is empty, then it is definitely gone. Return to the ocean any shell with a creature inside. Below are purchased shells which may or may not have been harvested before their time.

Baking Trays for Sorting

Just Lying There on a Bed of Casuarina Needles Waiting to be Admired

How Delightful to find a Sand Bar Without a Single Footprint

2. WHAT SUPPLIES DO YOU NEED?

Lamp

Choose a sturdy lamp to support and display your precious collection, not something that could easily be knocked over. Look for a rectangular lamp post set on a rectangular base. The base protects your lowest shells from breakage as the lamp is moved from place to place, or tipped to the side. Having said that, I myself have glued shells as far down the base as possible; I have learned to lift and move with care.

Why a rectangular post? Straight surfaces are easier to work with than rounded or uneven surfaces. I find that it's simply easier to place and glue shells in a pleasing arrangement. You may get more shells on a rectangular post, and the overall look may be more striking, I think. I strive for the look of abundance, something like a treasure chest from the sea. Pay attention to all surfaces. It may be possible to glue shells to the top of the post, and this continuous look can be pleasing, but

17

you will have to assess the ease of, say, pulling a chain to turn the light on; is there enough space to do that without hitting the shells and possibly damaging them? I prefer a lamp that turns on and off with a knob rather than a chain.

If the lamp has a finial above the shade, consider whether it will complement the overall look once your shell lamp is complete. If not, you may be able to purchase a different finial, or perhaps an appropriately sized shell could replace the existing finial.

Lampshade

You may or may not want to keep the shade that comes with the lamp. Once you have added shells to the post, the shade may no longer suit. For example, with the increased volume of the post, the shade may now be out of proportion with the rest of the lamp. It may be the wrong color, wrong material, or wrong design for the new look.

I work with an artist who makes jewelry and lampshades. Together we came up with a shade that compliments all of my shell lamps. The shade is large enough to accommodate the new dimensions of the post, and it is shaped in a way that enhances the look. She collects varieties of seaweed and incorporates them into her design. While the colors are somewhat intense at first, they fade over time, and eventually blend in beautifully with the post.

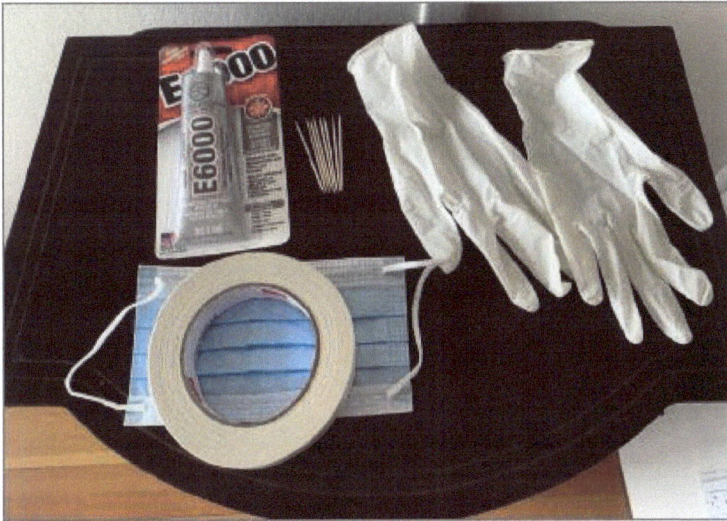

Glue

This is an extremely important part of the supply list. A strong and durable glue can prevent your precious pieces from falling off before the glue sets and can fortify your shells against the touch of curious hands. I use only E6000 glue because it is permanent and dries within 24 hours.

Since this glue is highly toxic, I work by an open window and I sometimes wear a light mask to cover my nose and mouth. You can rub some petroleum jelly or the like on the threads of the screw top for ease of opening and closing.

Pin

I use a straight pin to re-open the tip of the glue tube after the glue has set after my last use. Keep the tube cap handy to help contain the glue as you are working with it; the glue tends to overflow.

Working Surfaces

Your working surface needs to be sturdy. Be sure to protect it from the inevitable glue spillages. These days, I use a couple of folding craft tables, set up near a window, one for the lamp and one for the shells. It's nice to have an area dedicated for the purpose so you don't have to move or alter your work-station until you are finished your project.

Trays

I use baking trays to help sort my collection. I group my shells according to type, size, colour, function (some shells are fill-ers, some are the main feature of an area, some are foundation pieces). I sometimes set aside shells with a striking pattern or design so I can be sure to see it as I make selections for each side of the post. When you have a large collection, it can be difficult to remember all that you actually have. Being able to see at a glance all shells available for your lamp helps immensely in figuring out your design. Through experience, you will know which shell is likely to fit into a certain arrangement. Sometimes I decide in advance that I want to group, for example, all of my purple shells in one area on the lamp post. Presorting simplifies this process.

Gloves

These are essential for protecting your hands from glue. I use thin plastic gloves such as those used by my dental hygienist. I discard each pair after each work session. They get sweaty inside and may have glue on them, or tears, so don't try to reuse. There are times, however, when I find it's just too difficult to hold and manipulate a small shell into place while wearing slippery gloves. Fortunately, the recommended glue can be easily removed from fingers by rubbing them together and gathering up the pieces. Wash well with soap and water.
Wooden Toothpicks

I use a toothpick when I need to apply a small amount of glue. This is especially useful when gluing a very small shell or the fine structural details of a shell. You may also use a toothpick for scraping up excess glue or spills.

Tape and Scissors

Use painter's or masking tape to hold the shells in place, and scissors to cut the tape evenly. I find it convenient to pre-cut a few pieces of tape of varying sizes and adhere to the edge of the table for ease of access. For example, once you have positioned a shell and applied glue, it is awkward to have to unravel the spool of tape and cut to size; this is almost impossible if you are wearing gloves as the tape will stick to the gloves.

Freshly gathered and cleaned shells set out to dry. Notice shell fragments; if it catches your eye, bring it home.

Just a Quick Look, then Back into the Sea

Bubble Wrap

If your lamp post is square or rectangular, consider lying it flat on a table rather than working with the lamp in an upright position. Gravity will help keep the shells in place as the glue dries. This is especially useful if you are trying to glue on shells that are quite large.

Bubble wrap works beautifully for protecting shells from pressure as you turn the lamp to work on different sides of the post. I buy rolls of bubble wrap from Staples. I buy the one with the larger bubbles for greater protection and to better accommodate various shell sizes.

Cloth or Paper Towels

You need something to wipe up any glue spills immediately, before they begin to dry. As much as you might think that there won't be any spills, the glue oozes out of the tube even after you've finished squeezing the tube. I've learned to fit the cap back on loosely between applications just to catch the overflow.

One of my Favorite Sections

On this sandy shore we were delighted to find giant clam shells on the beach; a goat was tethered in the forest.

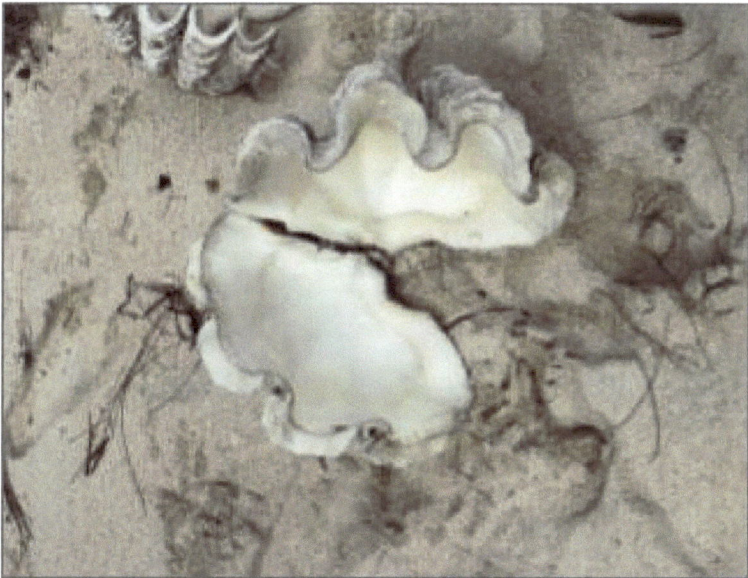

3. WHICH SHELLS ARE BEST?

That depends, in part, on the look you are aiming for; for example, do you prefer a delicate look with soft colors and lots of 'lace' (such as provided by tiny white branches, delicate corals, tiny bubble-like shells? You could seek out shine, bright colors, patterns, ridges, swirls. Do you want your lamp to be composed mainly of big, strong shells? shells of a specific type and only a few, if any, variations? or do you want your creation to be a mix of everything you have, arranged in the most esthetically pleasing way you can imagine?

There are no right answers to this question; it is mostly a matter of personal taste, and you may change your mind as you go along. Some hobbyists advocate placing the larger shells on the lower portion of the post, with a gradual climb towards the smaller, finer shells. Personally, I enjoy a much less structured approach. I sometimes try to start with a fairly consistent base; for example, a row of cockle shells. What goes above is whatever seems pleasing to my eye but, most importantly, I try to cover the underlying surface completely, wherever possible. For me, it's rather a willy-nilly approach, and I like it that way. It's fun to work without 'rules' sometimes, isn't it? When you allow yourself full freedom of creativity, amazing things can happen!

You may surprise yourself.

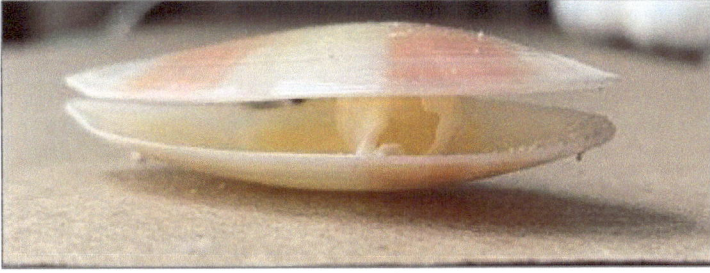

Sunrise tellin clam shells make excellent fillers but are also beautiful on their own. I love finding another shell stuck inside.

Embedded by Forceful Tides

Still only Shin Deep

4. MORE SUGGESTIONS

Shell Fragments

Many of my most gorgeous arrangements include pieces of shells fitted in so that they actually look whole. Incorporating a piece of shell with a striking design or a bright color can greatly enhance the overall aesthetic. Another advantage is that shell fragments can fill spaces where nothing else seems to fit.

I look for bright colors and often use fractured and misshapen shells.

Knowing this from the outset can simplify your shelling adventures. Imagine finding an eye-catching fragment that you would love to place on your lamp, then leaving it behind because the shell wasn't whole. Later on, as you are gluing shells to the post, you see a place where an attractive fragment could have been glued to fill that space, and really add to the overall look. Since it may not be easy to hop a plane and replay the scene, I tend to play it safe, not sorry, whenever I see anything that catches my eye.

As I comb the beaches, two of the things I look for are color and design. You may find a broken piece with an intriguing pattern or structure. You may find a piece that is a pretty shade of pink, or a bright butterfly yellow; maybe it catches your eye simply because it is shiny. One of my criteria for shelling is that the piece has to catch my attention in some way.

Fillers and Finishing Touches

I purposely collect certain shells that I know will make good fillers; for example, tiny shells can fill a slight gap in such a way that doesn't crowd a neighboring shell and hide more of the neighbor than intended.

Some shells are very useful as finishing touches. These are the pieces that you glue on last, such as those delicate white branches, and those tiny but whole pieces that are special in some way. Since they go on last, they will be clearly visible; they will be the 'frosting on the cake'. This is definitely one of my favorite parts of the shell lamp process.

Delicate Coral Branches make Beautiful Finishing Touches

Stars of the Show

Foundations

I agree that not all shells are interesting to look at. You may continually run across plain white shells that seem to be dull; not quite what you were looking for. However, shells like this can be very useful; in fact, I look at them as being 'practical shells. On my favorite beaches in the Caribbean, I can count on finding certain shells on certain beaches every trip.

Even when the pickings are slim, medium-sized, shiny white shells seem to be a staple on Tar Bay beach. They can serve as a foundation for other shells or as a bridge between shells. Being white, they fit in anywhere. The shiny white, delicate appearance of these shells reminds me of lightbulbs.

Size Matters

Large shells make your project easier because they cover a broader area. Tiny shells can be laborious to work with unless you like picky work, which I don't. If you are working on an area of tiny shells, I suggest you do a little bit at a time. That way, your mind can be refreshed and probably more creative when you resume work on that section.

I sometimes use a large shell as a foundation for smaller shells. There may be times, however, when you want to feature the large shell on its own. I suggest that you plan ahead, considering your intended overall look, when thinking about where to glue large shells. I use the word "intended" because plans often change along the way, and that's part of the fun.

Take some Time to Place and Consider

Sometimes I set aside a particular shell for a certain spot only to discover that it no longer fits the space available. Designing involves continual juggling and repositioning to find the right fit and the right look. In this case, I survey my collection again and make a more suitable choice. Indeed, it is rewarding to have a large collection from which to choose. The ability to be patient and flexible are good qualities to have when making a shell lamp.

Charming little Fish in the South Pacific

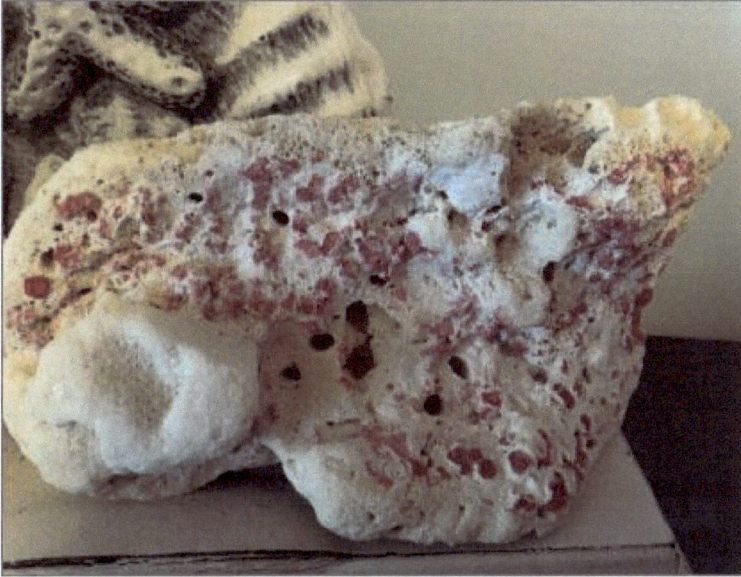

Corals can make Interesting and Colorful Additions to your Piece.

Corals

I often incorporate pieces of coral. Large and attractive pieces can cover a broad area, and coral is very strong, thus lending stability to your piece. Many corals are intricate in design, and these add interest and beauty. Corals used at the base of the lamp help support what goes above.

Foreign Objects

Previously, I mentioned the first time I saw a shell lamp. I was intrigued to find that the artist had placed a few tiny pearls in some double clam shells; it made me smile as I imagined her own enjoyment in doing this. It also made me think of other things that I might place in my own work. I could incorporate beach glass, for example; perhaps I could add small sea fans, or driftwood, or even stones that retained their color and design when dry. For me, these may be projects to look forward to. Right now, however, I love the look of an all-shell lamp, and I am looking forward to a different project involving beach stones and sea glass.

A Unique Shape Created over Time

Sharks

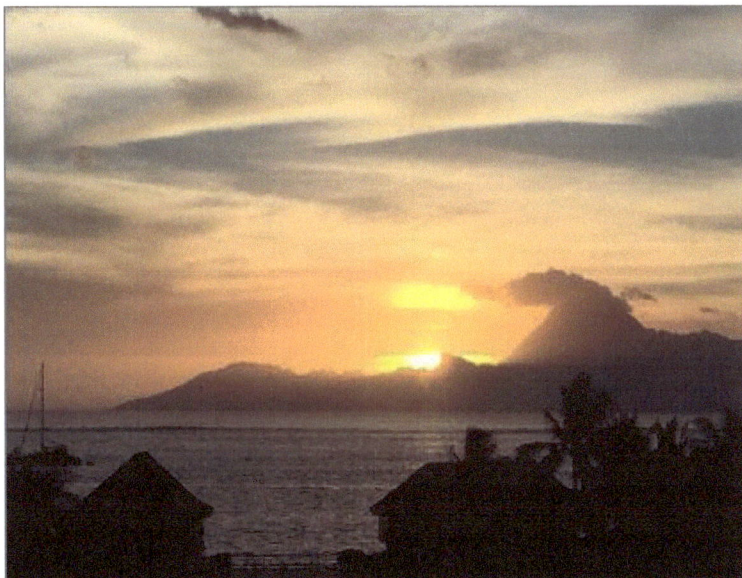

A Fire-Breathing Dragon in Tahiti at Sunset

5. START BUILDING YOUR LAMP

Organize your Shells

Up to this point, you have gone to a lot of work to collect, protect and transport your shells. You may find a lot of sand scattered about, so you may want to run some of your shells under water and dry them off. Clear your working surfaces of any grains of sand as well. I like to clean my shells before I come home, thus reducing the amount of sand carried forward. You can find tips on cleaning shells on the internet but, apart from soaking a sea urchin in vinegar, I find that a soft toothbrush and soap and water does a great job on most shells.

Organization Simplifies the Process

As mentioned under the Supply section, I find it very helpful to sort shells, especially if you have a large collection. This way, you are more likely to find quickly just the shell you need at just the right time. For example, sometimes you need to add color, or maybe you have a large space to fill; maybe you need a particularly strong piece for a vulnerable spot; maybe you need a tiny piece to fill a spot that wasn't fully covered by the shells you selected for a particular section.

Occasionally, you may finish your piece only to realize that you forgot your plan to feature a certain shell in a certain place. When focusing on the best fit for the pieces you are working with at the time, plans can dissipate. A somewhat organized collection may help you to remember your original intention.

When it comes time to add your finishing touches, a well-organized collection will help you see at a glance the location of your coral branches and your tiny starfish or sea urchins. These garnishes are not only fun but they complement your work and enhance the overall appearance. I also keep plenty of sunrise tellin clam shells handy.

Build from the Bottom Up

As mentioned previously, you might want to place your larger, heavier shells such as corals on the bottom. For my first lamp, I started with a row of cockle shells glued along the base on all sides. If you have enough of them, this arrangement can lend a pleasing consistency to your foundation.

Use the tube and/or a toothpick to apply a bit of glue on the shell and position it on the lamp. It doesn't require a lot of glue and, if you apply too much, the glue can ooze over the edges of the shell. I find the toothpick to be a good tool to scrape off the extra glue.

Positioning your Shells

Hold up a few shells to see if they fit the space available and the overall look of that section. This is an important and necessary part of the whole process, and there are usually a few surprises along the way. Take risks; they usually pay off.

It can be difficult to position and glue certain shells, depending on their structure. Sometimes there is only a thin edge to glue, and you may wonder if it will even stick. The most difficult gluing efforts occur when you cannot easily see which surface(s) of the shell will be contacting the lamp; sometimes you just have to guess and do your best. You will know the next day if you hit it right.

Once I position the glued shell to the lamp, I press and hold for a few seconds to help it set.

Place and Consider Before you Glue.

Testing Before Gluing

One of the most important things I can tell you about design-ing your shell lamp is to try and create 'movement'. If you glue all of your shells flat onto the surface of the lamp, you will end up with, well, another flat-looking surface. Instead, if you strive to have different levels of shells, some protruding out farther than others, you will end up with a more natural look. Think of the shells being swept in with the tide; a natural gathering of shells doesn't look flat, it has movement.

How can you create this look? I use less attractive shells for the foundation on which to prop the shells I want to feature. Most or all of the foundation will be hidden anyway. There are times, however, when part of the foundation shell is striking. You can position the foundation shell in such a way as to still show the best part of it while using the rest to raise up the other shell to create a more interesting look.

Layers of large Bubble Wrap Protect the most Fragile of Shells

Large Shells Fit Well at the Base

A Happy Sea Creature Unafraid of Tourists Bathing in the Shallow Water

Experiment until you get the Best Positioning and the Most Pleasing Aesthetic

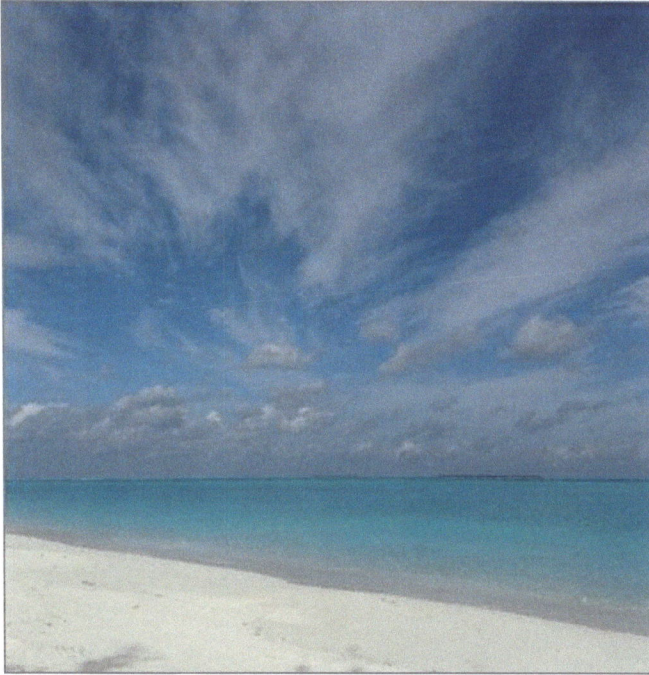

Rhapsody in Blue and White

Tape in Place

Now, once you have glued a few shells on your lamp, place some masking or painter's tape over the shells to hold them in place. If you plan to continue gluing beside the section you're working on, then pay attention to your tape placement. You don't want to end up having to remove tape in order to stick on more shells. Furthermore, try to avoid placing tape over a

61

starfish or other delicate shells that could break when you remove the tape. I know; sometimes your journey isn't predictable. Again, part of the fun.

Another plan might be to tape your lower section first then, while the glue is setting there, move on to the upper regions. In the upper region, you may decide to place some smaller shells. Whatever you choose to do, I can pretty much guarantee that your end result will be both surprising and beautiful.

After Gluing, Tape the Shells in Place until the Glue is Dry

Ensure that Shells are Secured

I like to begin work on my project in the morning, usually taking two days to complete each side. Although it takes 24 hours for the glue to dry, according to the package directions, you can actually resume work on that same side before the glue has fully dried.

After the shells are positioned and glued, then taped, I wait until the next day to check if the shells are secured; I do this by gently taping or pulling on the shell. Sometimes you have to re-glue, but this happens infrequently and usually it's because the joint was awkward. If it looks like it can't be done well, you may consider using a different shell.

Reposition the Lamp to its Vertical Position

I do this after each side is completed. When you work on a lamp that is lying flat on your working surface, you are working from a perspective that differs from the lamp's natural vertical position. You will see the obvious difference when you move the lamp to its upright position.

Now you may see gaps between shells that weren't at all obvious when the lamp was lying in its horizontal plane. One of the things I find most difficult is positioning, let's say, a shell that I have propped up on a foundation. If I glue the shell at a 45-degree angle while the lamp post is lying flat on the table, I may not be able to see the beautiful metallic green underside when the lamp is placed in its upright position. Usually, you have to glue at a much greater angle if you are to see your intended result.

Have Another Look

One of my favorite parts of this process is when all of my shells are placed and secured. This is the time for me to take 'one last look' and see if the overall appearance could be enhanced by the addition of, say, a starfish in just the right place, or that tiny red scallop shell that I couldn't find a place for before now. Now you may place those lacey white coral branches that hide gaps so well. They may not have been obvious to you when the lamp was lying down flat on your working surface.

Sunrise tellin clam shells, both singles and doubles, are marvelous for filling in gaps as they seem to fit in anywhere. Sometimes you have to angle them just right; sometimes you slide one end in and leave the other jutting out. You can count on this shell to make your arrangement look even better.

Consider the angle at which you place scallop shells when the lamp is lying flat; it will be different when you upright the lamp.

It's Fun to Nest Small Shells inside the Cup of Bigger Shells

This lamp fell to the floor and required repairing, which can be especially challenging. I have prepared a series of videos for sale demonstrating my process.

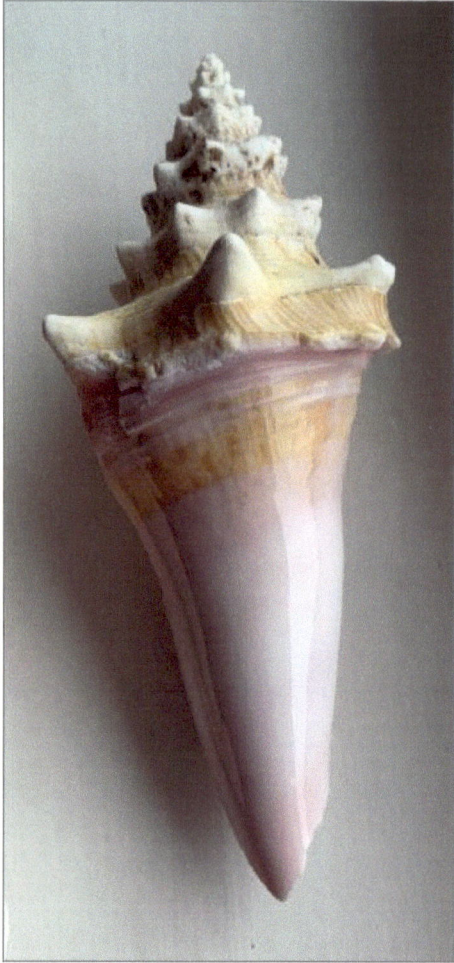

Conch Shell or Ice Cream Cone?

Look for interesting designs; if it catches your eye, bring it home (with permission).

6. A PICTURE IS WORTH A THOUSAND WORDS

I have taken photographs and videos throughout the process of building my most recent lamp, and hope that you would find them both useful and inspiring. The video series is extremely detailed, and some may enjoy watching and listening to the process in action more than reading about it. You can purchase the video series directly from my website: www.marenhill.com

The Markings on these Shells Remind me of Feathers.

Yes, I will Walk this Path.

Top Side or Under Side?

CONCLUSION

My creations may not be 'perfect', whatever that may be, but every time I look at them, they give me much pleasure. Not only do they look beautiful and enhance the room, but they remind me of so many good times spent on vacation with my husband. Memories fade with the passing of time, but your work and play in completing a seashell lamp will undoubtedly become the gift that keeps on giving throughout the years.

Thank you for purchasing my books and videos.
Happy shelling!

Turquoise Water + Powdery White Sand = Paradise

Each Lamp Post Displays your Own Unique Creation, Different every Time

Keeping Doubles Intact can be Tricky

Like the Wings of an Angel

Gorgeous even when Cloudy

Iconic Over-Water Beach Huts in Morea

Looking out from Hydra at sunset

ABOUT THE AUTHOR

Best-selling author, J.D. Monk, is an avid collector of seashells and other beach treasures.

She is the author of a children's book, *Slimy Slick*, novels *Nicole*, and *The Troublemakers* by Maren Hill, her pen name. ***Casuarina House*** is to follow.

Find out more about JD Monk and her new releases on her website at www.marenhill.com

JD Monk/Maren Hill's books can be ordered through all major bookstores and through Amazon.

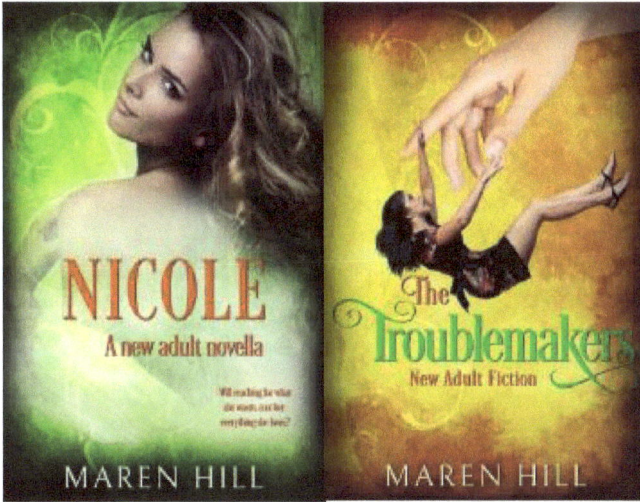

J.D. Monk with her Most Recently Completed Lamp